MW01296075

BACK IN THE TIME

Medicine, Education and Life
In the Isolation of Western North Carolina's
Spring Creek

Jasper B Reese

JASPER BERNIE REESE

WITH GRETCHEN GRIFFITH

Gretchen Griffith

Back in the Time:
Medicine, Education and Life
In the Isolation of Western North Carolina's Spring Creek

BACK IN THE TIME: Medicine, Education and Life in the Isolation of Western North Carolina's Spring Creek
Copyright © 2017 Jasper B. Reese & Gretchen Griffith
All rights reserved.

Printed in the United States of America

All rights reserved solely by the authors. The authors guarantee all contents are original and do not infringe upon the legal rights of any other person or work. No part of this book may be reproduced in any form without the permission of the authors. The views expressed in this book are not necessarily those of the publisher.

Library of Congress Control Number: 2017902498
CreateSpace Independent Publishing Platform, North Charleston, SC

Non-Fiction/Memoir/Biography
Cover designs: Gretchen Griffith and Tina Bryant
Front cover photo – From the personal collection of J. B. Reese
Back cover photo – Courtesy of Spring Creek Community Center

Unless otherwise credited, interior photos are from the authors' personal collections.

Preface

Originally I set out to write this as a gift to my family, but I soon realized these stories about a way of life too often lost in our fast-paced, high tech, modern civilization need to be shared with everyone. Being isolated in the mountain culture of the Spring Creek community of North Carolina's Madison County presented challenges to all of us who were fortunate enough to call this spot on earth home.

Gifford Pinchot, a pioneer in forest management at Biltmore Forest, spent quite a bit of time in Madison County during the turn of the twentieth century, observing not only the land, but the families who lived here. He noted that even though some of them had absolutely nothing, they were the most independent people he had ever seen. Indeed, all our ancestors at some time had no modern conveniences, yet they thrived on their own, despite hardships.

It was a good time to live when a man's word was his bond, and a handshake as good as a written contract. The value of honesty, discipline and respect for God and our fellow men was passed down through generations. I tell in this book of a togetherness, a cohesive force necessitated by conditions back in the time that brought out the best in people who were self-sufficient, innovative and industrious. This was a real and natural, down-to-earth true way of life that I knew growing up, both the good parts of it and the bad. They shouldn't be forgotten.

I am especially grateful to my co-author, Gretchen Griffith, whose encouragement and literary ability helped make this book a reality.

Jasper Bernie (J. B.) Reese

Dedication

Helen Whisnant Reese
Thanks for all the great memories

Dedicated to my wife, Helen,

Posthumously to my mother,
Nola Plemmons Reese,

All my grandmothers,

And all the women like them who are fighting for
their equal rights under the law

Table of Contents

Spring Creek

Chapter One
Up the Creeks:
The Land

Back in the time of the early twentieth century — The place is the southwestern corner of western North Carolina's Madison County, a southern Appalachian bit of high country isolated by the quirks of nature.

More specifically, this is a high valley shaped like an oblong, flat bottomed bowl with layers upon layers of surrounding mountains along its rim setting it apart from the rest of the world. The entire area is delineated by Spring Creek, into which all other local branches and underground springs that bubble to the surface eventually flow. Spring Creek originates thousands of feet above sea level in the watershed at Betsy's Gap at the Madison-Haywood county line. Being on the western slopes of the Eastern Continental Divide, water that dribbles downhill from here finds its way into the Mississippi River. First it must flow northward past four combination post office-country stores that are the center of several local communities.

The first community downstream is Luck by name, then on to Trust where the drainage off Doggettt Mountain and Friezeland confluence to swell Spring Creek even more. Atop Doggettt Mountain is a small community we call Sliding Knob in the winter and Mt. Pleasant in the summer, the reasons easily apparent. Forever seeking the lowest point, the water rushes down the steep mountainsides only to meander slowly through this long valley known as the Flats of Spring Creek. It continues beyond the Spring Creek Post Office, then past another at Bluff, drops through a deep gorge where the road clings on the edge of a thousand foot cliff, cascades down the side of Hot Springs Mountain at the Van Cliffs, flows through the town of Hot Springs where it spills into the French Broad River. In its seventeen odd miles journeying from source to mouth, it is swollen by side streams with names such as Roaring Fork, Little Creek, Long Branch, Baltimore Branch and Panther Branch. It's on one of those tributaries where I am born, 1930, in the community known as Joe with its combination post office and store on the banks of Meadow Fork, a major stream, second largest to Spring Creek. The electric lines and hard surfaced roads end fifteen miles away, and fifteen hundred feet lower in elevation.

I spend a lot of my early years walking along the streams of Madison County with the mountains around me attempting to set my limits. No matter which direction I turn, I face towering mountains that contain the valley. From the top of the mountains towards the southwest at Maple Springs and Cold Springs, all the creeks flow into the Pigeon River as a part of the eastern continental divide. Water there flows west through a gorge and into the French Broad in Tennessee and eventually into the Mississippi River. However, all water on my side of the mountain flows into Spring Creek and then the French Broad where it joins with the waters from the Pigeon River to empty into the Tennessee River and then the great Mississippi.

To the west, the valley is bounded by the backbone of the Blue Ridge at the Tennessee line. A footpath that later becomes the Appalachian Trail rides its spine and goes either southward past the Cold Springs National Forest to the terminus in Georgia, or on and on northward to end in the state of Maine. Locally this pedestrian-only trail winds down a two thousand foot drop in elevation to Hot Springs from higher peaks of mountains often referred to as the Bald Mountains, and its most noted bald, Max Patch, a phenomena named

The view from atop Max Patch

because no trees grow on the land. While many balds are naturally occurring, Max Patch supposedly is not. It was cleared in the late nineteenth century for farmers seeking high pastures for their cattle in the heat of the summer, because at an elevation well over four thousand feet above sea level, days are much cooler here. Supposedly the name Max derives from the local Scottish settlers with surnames that begin Mac or Mc. A more shortened, casual way to speak of a man in these years is to call him Mac. Since this is a part or patch of Mac's land, it becomes known as Mac's Patch and the spelling evolves into Max Patch. The community locals simply call it "The Patch."

It is not the highest in elevation of the mountains surrounding it, but it is high enough that on clear days, the isolation forced on those of us living in this part of the world is apparent. The Smoky Mountains lie to the south, and to the east, the highest peak this side of the Mississippi River, Mount Mitchell, makes travel and communication extremely difficult.

Big Bald stands to the north, and to the west, Tennessee with its many mountains. The cliffs on these mountainsides block out sunlight below and the steep slopes make farming near to impossible. Near, but not impossible.

Max Patch is grass-covered unlike most of the surrounding mountain tops. At over four thousand feet elevation, it offers a three hundred sixty degree view of the surrounding landscape, and an eighteen hundred foot long flat top on which small single engine bi-wing planes land in the thirties and forties. During these years, it is also the favorite place for outdoor recreation for young and old alike. We go there often, pack a lunch and drive all the way up to the top to picnic in the grass. Daddy plays ball with us there. Max Patch is the setting for wrestling matches, small carnival acts, horseback competition among local men, picnics, weddings, preaching and singing events, and of course, hiking. The Appalachian Trail crosses the top of Max Patch near the Tennessee state line.

Around three or four hundred feet from the top, between Max Patch and a ridge below it known as the Buckeye, water bubbles up from the earth into the grass. This is the spring that forms the headwaters of Roaring Fork. The Reese family owned the Buckeye when my father was young, and ran sheep on it. His chore was to remain at the spring overnight to kill wild dogs before they killed the sheep. My Uncle Gonnie claims this is one of the boldest springs he has ever seen.

Springs develop because of capillary action. The earth is like a sponge or a piece of paper towel thrown in water that pulls the liquid into it. Soil does the same thing, absorbs the water and holds it until it gushes over. A spring as we define it is where this absorbed water comes out of the underground. Springs are so important to our existence that we assign them names, and designate them as landmarks for references.

North of Max Patch is Bluff Mountain in the Pisgah National Forest. Because of the abundance and beauty of natural growing wildflowers around the mountain, people refer to it as the "Gardens of Bluff." Nearby are other prominent peaks Lamb's Knob and Big Bald, the tallest peak in the Bald Mountains at an elevation of five thousand five hundred sixteen feet. Several mountains in this range have grassy balds similar to the one at Max Patch.

Before 1921 — Paths first carved into the land by buffalo and elk seeking water or summer grasses or winter shelter, are followed by the Cherokees and later by the early Scotch Irish settlers. These primitive roads often parallel the creeks around them, fording them several times, and even following them midstream when necessary.

The state of North Carolina establishes an unpaved, standard width road between Lake Junaluska to the south of Spring Creek and Hot Springs to the north, and assigns it State Highway number #209. The road divides the flats long ways into two equal halves and reroutes into the center of the flats away from the original Spring Creek School on the eastern side of the valley.

1929 — After several years of construction, the final leg of Highway #209 from Hot Springs to Bluff is completed. Jimmy Council of Boone, North Carolina has been the engineer in charge of the project with Tony Anzas as construction superintendent.

1954 — State Highway #209 is paved.

1990 — In an attempt to showcase the state's "breathtaking scenery" the North Carolina Department of Transportation selects specific scenic routes throughout the state and designates them as scenic byways.

April 4, 1997 — The North Carolina Scenic Byway Program adds State Highway #209 to the list. Because of the rich history of music in the region, where singing is as natural as breathing, its formal name becomes "The Appalachian Medley."

2009 — Business owner James Ferguson is riding in a car from Hot Springs to his store at the intersection of Highway #209 and Max Patch Road. "Don't talk to me," he warns the driver. "I'm going to count the curves."

The trip begins at the French Broad River and he counts every curve, every turn the car makes. The twenty-four mile trip up the escarpment, through the flats and around even more mountain sides, according to his count, contains a whopping two hundred ninety curves.

This Harley Davidson enthusiast later is riding the nearby "Tail of the Dragon" Highway from North Carolina into Tennessee with its three hundred eighteen curves, all the time thinking Highway #209 needs an equally exciting name. After several possible title suggestions, he finally dubs it "The Rattler," not only because of its frequent "S" shaped curves, but also because of an image he remembers from his childhood. When the road was being paved, he watched every evening as the construction workers brought at least two or three dead rattlesnakes from their daily encounters.

His son, Mark Ferguson, has registered the title of the road to include the full length from Hot Springs to Lake Junaluska. Items specific to ®*The Rattler* are for sale in Ferguson Supply at the intersection of Highway #209 and Max Patch Road.

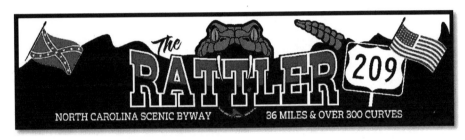

®*The Rattler banner courtesy of Mark Ferguson and Jason Swope*

Along Spring Creek at Trust

Chapter Two
Roots Along the Creeks:
My People

Back in the time, centuries ago — I come from two families long established in Madison County, Reese on my father's side, and Plemmons on my mother's.

The Reese family is from Wales, arriving here under the original name's spelling Rhys. One of my ancestors, Travis Reese, in 1740 comes from South Carolina into what is Wilkes County, North Carolina. His oldest son, Tom, serves alongside him in the Revolutionary War and they move into Madison County some time before the Civil War. Mostly their persuasion during that conflict is with the north and there is a meeting they attend at the Poplar Gap Church of the ones who were trying to dodge conscription. The Seventh Confederate Army will come looking, and anybody fourteen or fifteen years old or up, they will take them. If they aren't old enough to put on the battlefield, they will put them to work. The first doctor in our family is Martin Van Buren Reese, who as family lore tells, gets his medical degree through an apprenticeship from a northern doctor during the Civil War.

Grandpa Moses Reese and family. Dad is the baby in Grandma's lap.
Two more boys come later.

There is a big Reese family of my daddy's daddy, the Reverend William Reese, more commonly known as Preacher Billy Reese. My Grandma Reese is a Strickland by birth. Their family comes into Madison from North Carolina's Watauga County in the 1880's.

My great, great-grandfather on my mother's side, Daniel Keener, is from Germany, the first of his family that comes over. His grandson Jess is my Grandma Plemmons' father. Grandpa Jess, I call him even though he is my great-grandfather, is a big man with a beard down to here. He was a cook in the Civil War. His brother Martin Keener, the last anyone knows of him, was sitting on a rail fence crying and the family suspected some Yankees from Tennessee captured him when he would not join the Confederate Army.

Jess Keener and his wife Matilda Brown Keener

My great-grandparents, Harriet and James Newton Plemmons,
but I called him Pap

Great-grandma Harriet surrounded by her Keener family

The Plemmons triplets:
Dora (Hicks), Zora (Carpenter) and my mother, Nola (Reese)

1930 — The typical person in this section of Madison County works his farm, goes to church, obeys the law and raises his family. As self-sufficient and individualistic as my people are, we are united with others of their community through faith. Each community has at least one church, mostly Baptist, but also Salvation Army and a few Methodist through their circuit riders. Each community has a church building close by within walking distance. The preacher comes on Saturday and stays overnight with someone in the community and preaches the next day. He spends the night on Sunday as well if anybody invites him to stay. Some churches do have ministers living locally.

Mountain beliefs tend to be strict constructionist with scripture superseding man-made law. Preachers have a strong missionary zeal and ample fire and brimstone sermons that teach the value of honesty, discipline and respect for God and each other. A man's word is his bond and a handshake is as good as a written contract.

Church is the major and most frequent place for recreation and romance. This is where boy meets girl at night time prayer meeting and revival meetings. (Paw can't see who is walking daughter home in the dark.) The church is also the place for reunions, decorations, gospel group singing and weddings. And the summer Bible school.

Tradition dictates that on Decoration Day members of a family decorate the graves of their ancestors and essentially hold a homecoming, reunion, and decorating in one. The whole community gets back together for the decoration. Those who have moved away return for the day. Decoration Day at Keenerville is the third Sunday in August and the one at Poplar Gap the second Sunday in September.

My people also get together to participate in assisting others needing help with large projects such as building a house and barn for newlyweds or clearing the woods off a few acres so it can be farmed. This event is known as a "working" although it turns out to be also recreational in nature.

A "working" to clear land of trees begins at first light with the arrival of men with teams of big horses, steers, or mules to pull and pile the bigger logs for sawing into lumber, to pull stumps out of the ground. The closest thing to machinery that can work these steep slopes and ridges is a team of mules pulling a turning plow. Men bring sharp cross-cut saws and double bitted axles to cut down trees and trim brush and cut surface roots so the stumps can be pulled. These incoming teams usually are pulling a wagon or sled with the women and children. Some are riding and some are walking alongside, bringing the food: fried chicken, ham, backbone and ribs, beans, potatoes, cornbread and biscuits "made from scratch," chocolate, apple and cherry pies, chocolate and coconut cakes and lots of each; enough for dinner and supper! After all, this "working" is a daylight to dark operation.

This is a festive occasion full of friendly competition and boasting. "My horses are the best."

"I can chop bigger chips and get that tree to fall exactly where I want it better than anybody."

"You should see the size of the pig I fattened up for hog killing time."

Telling tall tales and boasting is a way of entertainment to the mountain man. His tall tales and boasting are usually so ridiculous that everyone understands this is just having fun.

My grandpa Plemmons told about a man who traveled to California and had seen the redwood trees. He came back to Madison County telling the true story about a tree that was so enormous, someone had cut a tunnel out of its inside big enough to drive a bus through. A logger by trade, Grandpa thought a few minutes and said, "That's nothing. A huge tree fell across the tracks not too long ago. The train's brakes failed and it ran partially into that tree and cut a tunnel big enough for small cars to drive through, and then skipped the tracks, drove along inside the tree and came out through a knothole!"

Nothing is more important to the average Madison man than his individuality, his self-confidence, his self-sustaining life style, his pride in his availability to go it alone if necessary and his honesty and truthfulness...with those tall tale exceptions. However, politics has no place at these "workings." That is for other days.

When the land is cleared, it is called a "new ground," there is usually a little "shine" available before supper as a way of celebrating a long day of hard work, fun and success! The scriptures control the drink. "BE MODERATE IN ALL YE DO" on these occasions. Some of the deacons are there!

The thirties — The United States of America and the whole world, for that matter, is in the Great Depression. However, most people of Madison do not pay much attention to it. They have always been depressed economically, but don't know it, being self-sufficient, independent people. Like the generations before them, they depend on small farms and whatever else the mountains and streams could provide for survival, working the land the best way they can. A family might be living in somebody else's old run down abandoned house, not owning a cow or anything of value, living off the fat of the land, which can be done in the mountains. Three of the seasons always offer food of some sort for those who are industrious enough to gather it.

Before fertilizers come along, the farmer clears a plot of land and uses it several years until it can no longer support healthy crops. He turns that into pasture land and clears another section.

This so-called "FAT OF THE LAND" produces much food and some money. There are many berries and fruits for the picking; strawberries, blackberries, huckleberries grow wild in abundance. If a person is big enough to walk and carry a gallon bucket, he (or she) is big enough to pick fruit, and forced to do so! Also, there are apple and cherry trees scattered throughout the area with plenty more chores waiting.

Tobacco is one cash crop that brings in some money, bright leaf tobacco sold at markets near Biltmore, east of Asheville and in Greenville, Tennessee. Farmers take their crops there to huge warehouses where the auctioneers sell baskets of tobacco filled to the brim.

The most fertile, best laying half acre or so, usually located close to the house, is reserved for the family garden where all kinds of vegetable are grown. The women of the house preserve several hundred jars of vegetables, fruits, juices, and jelly each summer by canning them in glass jars. The canned goods are kept from freezing by placing them in a

Uncle Tony Plemmons, the tobacco farmer of the family, and the last of ten brothers and two sisters. He lives to be a hundred years old and is the patriarch of the Keenerville community.

dug out space under the house. Potatoes are preserved by digging a hole in the garden, lining it with straw, filling it with potatoes, and covering the hole with a big mound of dirt. No one goes hungry in Madison County during the Great Depression if they will work!!

Only the kitchen and living room are heated, so the bedrooms are very cold in winter. The solution is lots of quilts. Scrap cloth of all kinds is saved to be sewn into the quilt tops. The inside is cotton stuffing, and white cotton cloth covers the bottom. One can never have too many quilts, so the women join together in quilting parties. When couples get married they need quilts!

Most of our clothing is home-made, especially women's and girl's wear. Most all women are good seamstresses by necessity. They also knit and embroider. With no electricity, they hand stitch, or sew on pedal driven Singer treadle machines. Local stores stock wide rolls of bolted cloth of different color and design. A popular and inexpensive source of cloth for dresses and underclothes is cotton sacks containing a supply of feed for animals or flour for cooking. Once the contents are used, the material is available to design into clothing. The Brand & Shorts feed sacks come in three different colors and patterns while flour sacks are solid white except for a red rooster in a circle on one side.

I am about nine or ten years old and a girl in my class comes home with me from Sunday School one summer day. We are playing summersault in the yard and her dress flies up. There on her butt is that flour sack red rooster. There is a slang expression chanted by us boys: "Flat Foot Floogie with the flour sack drawers."

We have about as good a life as any family living through the thirties and the Great Depression. Like all other families in this isolated region, we have learned to survive the elements by using our intelligence. Outsiders cannot determine from how isolated a person is, what his brain power is. Those of us who are secluded and isolated are not ignorant. True, we are ignorant of what we do not know, just as everyone is ignorant to some degree. We have good minds and problem solving abilities. A farmer that must repair broken equipment himself because he has no access to a store uses his intelligence. We have unlimited proof that the people that come from these secluded areas do well even after they move away and are exposed to modern information. This gets back to the old problem, a little psychology, sociology, and the argument, "Are you what you are because of who you are or more because of where you are?"

In order for a farmer to be successful, he has to be innovative. He has to be smart to succeed because if he breaks something, he doesn't have a repair shop nearby. He is constantly inventing new approaches, new ways to solve his problems. He is not, as the saying goes, like one that just gets off the cabbage truck. These people who are isolated in their own environments are very intelligent. Anyone who can successfully survive the Great Depression of 1930's without any modern conveniences can survive anywhere!

During the forties — Grandpa Plemmons and his wife Laura move to Caldwell County, North Carolina where he opens a store on the Collettsville Road.

Chapter Three
Mountain Medicine:
My Father's Story

Back in the year 1919 — My grandfather Plemmons is on a logging job over in Cataloochee in the Big Creek section. He comes down with a bad case of the influenza that is spreading across the nation, and he will die without help from old Doc Peck. There are many older people in poor health as well as sick babies living there in Big Creek's temporary housing, the slab shacks provided for the workers and their families. To help those who are sick with the flu, the lumber company ships in prebuilt houses on the same narrow gauge railroad they use to haul logs out. These houses are delivered on a flat railroad car, and the workers use skid poles around the frames to slide them off sideways. Grandpa is moved into one of the new houses along with other men, many who are bedfast with flu. At least they are now out of the weather and away from the snow blowing through the cracks in the wall.

The treatment is to keep a patient dry and warm, and if he can live long enough to wait it out, and is strong enough, he survives. If not, he dies. Those developing pneumonia face the same prognosis, if a patient lives long enough to put a mustard plaster on his chest and cloths on his head, he lives.

Dr. Frisbee, photograph courtesy of the Frisbee family and the Spring Creek Community Center

One of the earliest doctors in the mountain communities is Dr. Frisbee, who makes his rounds on the only transportation available, horseback.

1930 — My dad is a Registered Nurse practicing medicine as an apprentice under Dr. David Kimberly at Hot Springs serving the Spring Creek communities. He is working on his medical degree.

The main obstacles to getting medical care are the harsh winter weather, very few automobiles on even worse unpaved roads, lack of communication, and no electricity. Subzero temperatures on top of snow and ice for days at a time are not unusual. Winters are especially deadly on older people and babies with pneumonia, fever, flu, or appendicitis. Antibiotics like sulfur drugs and penicillin will not become available until after World War II.

All too often, when people get seriously ill they either recover on home remedies or die. The most popular cough medicine is a little moonshine mixed with brown sugar. Other home remedies are mustard poultices for a raw congested chest, blackberry wine to lower high fever, or sassafras tea for stomach problems.

As tough as it is for men under these primitive conditions, it is much tougher for the women. The life expectancy of a woman is considerably less than that of a man due to her hard way of life. On average women have a baby about every two to three years that supplies the men with a labor force for farm chores. She is expected to do all the housework with no conveniences, no electricity, no water in the house, and washing clothes on an old rub board outside in all kinds of bad weather. Housework of any nature is beneath the dignity of a man who risks ridicule by friends if they suspect him of doing housework.

1931 — Dad has to cut his practice short and return north to John Hopkins and Massachusetts General for more medical training. What he has to endure there while getting his medical education! Daddy not only does all his school work, but he also works in the lunchroom. The more well-to-do boys turn up their noses at him when he carries their plates, for example.

During these back to school periods there is no doctor to be had for the most part in back country of Madison County since Dr. Kimberly works mostly in the Hot Springs area.

1935 and I am five years old before I first remember seeing my dad. He comes back to Madison County and starts his medical practice again, a year or so at a time, returning to school frequently for more training. We move to a three-roomed house in the village near the Bluff post office-store combination.

Dad brings home potatoes, hams, or all kinds of food instead of cash for his services. However, this one particular time he shows up with a Billy goat complete with a harness and a wagon. There's also a jug of shine involved because Dad comes home riding in the wagon, pulled by the goat and feeling no pain! We kids have a ball playing with that goat and wagon until the goat becomes so mean he turns dangerous! When he isn't hooked to the wagon, he tries to get even with us for what we have done to him while he is pulling us around! Dad finally gives the goat to a hungry family. When my dad, as the country doctor for this area, goes on a call, he sometimes does not return home for several days. He stays with pneumonia patients until the fever breaks or until he is called from that patient to see yet another one and then another one, at somewhere else. This continues for days where he is taken from patient to patient and back again to the first one without returning to our home. There are no telephones to contact us and reassure my mother that he is safe.

My father, Bernie Eugene Reese

Dad getting his exercise while at medical school

Communication for emergencies to alert the doctor is made by one of the few people who has a car, usually an A model Ford, or by someone riding horseback to our house at Bluff. Frequently the patient's family lives in an open secluded cove of farmable land only accessible through a narrow hollow from the road. In these cases, a horse or a mule is led out to the road for the doctor to ride in. Their family horse or mule is the transport my dad must use to get to his most isolated patients. These situations are the same, summer, winter, sunshine or flood. It makes no difference.

Any time my dad is on a call in the area of Maple Springs on the Max Patch Road, he stops in the Salvation Army's Mountain Mission, gives the children their shots and treats any who are sick. He will also leave medicine for future use or send some back to them when he doesn't have enough in his bag. During one of these visits he discovers his own deceased sister's daughter living at the school. She had been abandoned by her father who lived nearby at Popular Gap. Dad takes her home with him to live with us and enrolls her in Spring Creek High School where she can finish her education.

1940 and I am ten years old — While cutting the Dock-root up with my razor-sharp ax so it would dry more quickly on the tin roof, I become distracted and cut my left thumb almost completely off! Lucky for me, Dad is home at the time. He grabs his medical bag and gets my thumb back in place and the bleeding stops. He then gets a neighbor with a car to take us to Dr. Kimberly's clinic in Hot Springs. They put me to sleep with ether and sew the thumb back together. When I wake I have two sore places! While I am asleep they circumcise me!

It is also election season where a liberal supply of "shine" becomes available to both sides on Election Day and causes both "high old times" and fist fights. Madison medical care gets mixed up in politics in sort of a superficial way when my dad plays a political game during the campaign for local officials. He carries absentee ballots in his pocket as a convenience for the many bedfast patients and others who are living back in the coves and are too busy or not all that interested in politics anyway. They trust his judgment to cast their votes for them. He is a "died-in-the-wool" liberal married to a staunchly conservative woman raised by my Grandpa Plemmons. Dad thinks the president, FDR, is second only to the powers that be, so the conservatives hate to see him coming.

December 7, 1941 — We get alarming news on our battery powered radio. The Japanese sneak attack on Pearl Harbor makes everybody fighting mad! All able-bodied men eighteen to twenty-five years of age either volunteer or are drafted into military service during World War II. Although Dad is thirty-five years old, he is determined to go to war. However, he cannot pass the strict physical examination for a commission

since he had Rheumatic fever as a child that left him with a bad heart. He tries to enlist three times before he is accepted. Because of his medical abilities, they finally take him in the Navy and promote him to the highest enlisted rank of Chief Petty Officer. He is assigned to a Seabees unit and sent to the South Pacific Theater of Operations where his unit is pinned down in fox holes by the Japanese for several days on one of the islands. He catches malaria fever and his heart condition gets worse.

During the war both he and Dr. Kimberly serve in the armed forces and there is no doctor available for the people of this backcountry until Dr. Mason opens a medical practice out of Bluff. The closest hospital is over thirty miles away in Asheville.

Bernie Reese with Dr. Kimberly

Dr. Mason, photograph courtesy of Spring Creek Community Center

1944 — My father is discharged with forty percent disability because of the malaria from his war duty. He is never able to carry on his medical practice in the mountains for long periods of time after that and is in and out of the VA hospitals several times. He immediately gets a great paying and traveling job with the Sterling Drug Company. Since only the military had the use of the new antibiotic drugs during the war, Dad has had firsthand experience using them. His job is to travel through Midwestern states and demonstrate the use of these new wonder drugs to hospitals, doctors and other medical personnel. He has an unlimited expense account for travel and hotels, so one summer he takes this fourteen year-old never-been-any-where boy with him, first to St Louis, Missouri, then to Omaha, Nebraska. We travel first class in the new streamlined trains. We visit the zoo in St. Louis. We ride a roller-coaster. We stay in the best hotels where he rents an entire suite and invites all the medical people to demonstrate the new antibiotics' uses. While we are in Omaha I get a job in a little hole-in-the-wall hamburger café named The Tom Thumb.

After a few weeks Dad sends for Mom and moves the family to Omaha. However, we all get homesick for the mountains and move back to Madison County.

1946 — Dad begins his medical practice again. He and my mother buy land on Spring Creek and start building a large brick house. They select the plans from the *Better Homes and Gardens Magazine*. However, no carpenters or masons in our area can read the plans! We finally find an old gentleman in Haywood County by the name of Frank Davis who can read them. We all call him Uncle Frank. Dad puts him in charge of the building, the hiring and the firing. He moves in and lives with us until the building is complete. He is a tough task master! He works me all day mixing concrete by hand and then, because he is crippled in his right leg, leans heavy on this sixteen-year-old as we walk a half mile to the house we are renting at the time. I develop the greatest admiration and respect for Uncle Frank even though for some unknown reason he calls me James all the time! He works us hard from sun up to sun down, but, he works as hard as any of us, and in pain from that lame leg most of the time. We do not have electricity yet, but we do know that the REA (the Rural Electrical Administration) is coming soon, so we wire the house as we build it. In the meantime, a lot of the hand sawing and hand mixing concrete must take place!

We spend many hours hunting with Dad's favorite hounds

Hot Springs, the closest town, is twelve to fifteen miles away from us and has a little theatre that on Saturdays will often show western movies. A bunch of us boys try to get loose from doing work about noon, and harder yet, get money from someone to get a hamburger, Pepsi and movie fare. I have two major problems. Dad is busy night and day in his mountain medical practice, either out of the house on calls or trying to get some sleep and rest. If he is home, I don't dare wake him to get money! So, I have to convince Uncle Frank that I am going to quit working anyway at noon whether he lends me a measly dollar or not! After good many threats back and forth, the old rascal blows out deep breaths three or four times through the side of his mouth, and then very slowly takes out a roll and sees if he can find a one among the hundreds! He always comes through after several lectures on savings and safety and I learn to love the old rascal!

While we are building the house, Dad rents an office from a distinguished widow there in the community, a Mrs. Hunter, the same lady he once boarded with to attend school. Because there is no electricity available to run a refrigerator, she allows him to store certain medicines in the gas powered refrigerator of her home.

Once we move into the new house, Dad uses one of the rooms he specifically built to be his office. Although seventy-five percent of his patients are bedfast with no way of transportation for them to get to him, he does have a good number of patients come to the office. Even so, he continues his home visits to serve the majority of his patients.

1950 — My father takes a position on the staff of Massachusetts General Hospital in Boston as Director of the Nursing Department. They sell the brick house they had built in Spring Creek and he and my mother move to Boston to an apartment in a complex in Beacon Hill. One summer he hires my brother as a ward boy.

1952 — The Veteran's Administration declares him 100% disabled and he is forced to retire.

March, 1954 — Major Cecil Brown of Maple Springs Salvation Army Mountain Mission and a great friend with my father through the years, preaches his funeral at Keenerville Church. He is a few months short of forty-eight years of age. The harsh mountain medical practice and being pinned down in a foxhole for days in World War II are life shorteners for him, that, and the fact he is a chain smoker. The day of his funeral there is so much snow and ice on Long Branch Road we are unable to get the hearse to take him up the mountain to his home church, the elementary school and cemetery at Popular Gap. He is buried instead at the church cemetery in Keenerville.

The graveyard behind the church at Keenerville

Riding along the flats of Spring Creek

**Chapter Four
My Story:
From Isolation to Success**

Back in the time, 1930 — I come squalling into the world on May seventeenth, my father's first boy! I am later told he celebrated with a jug of "shine" while riding his grey mare through the hallway of the old farm house several times! I am named after my father and my mama's father. His name is Jasper Newton and mine is Jasper Bernie, my middle name from my daddy, Bernie Eugene Reese.

The house we are living in is a one room, plank house beside my Grandpa Plemmons' big two-story farm house, about a hundred feet between the houses. He builds it for Mama, my sister Cleo Marie and me to live near him while Dad is in school. Grandpa's bee stands, cherry trees, spring and spring-house are between his back door and our little house. This is a long walk for a three year old every morning to get his breakfast. I have to get down on all hands and feet to crawl up the steps into the kitchen door where I find Grandpa waiting by the old wood cookstove while Grandma cooks the best bread and gravy I ever tasted! He gets me on his lap and pretends to steal a biscuit for me from the pan on the oven door.

Grandpa Plemmons is a great man, more like a father to me since mine is away at medical school. From him, I get my first name, Jasper. He loves hunt with his pack of fox hounds, and as I grow older, he takes me with him some times. We meet with other fox hunters, climb one of the higher mountains at night, build a big fire, sit around it and listen to the dogs chase a fox.

We have no electricity and we are too far away for delivery of ice to maintain an icebox. We grow our own food and preserve it for use during the entire year. In order to keep our canned food from freezing and bursting the jars, we bury them in a dug-out or a tunnel under the house. To keep milk and butter or anything else cool in summer, we have a spring-house, a small shed, six by eight feet in size, built over the location where the spring gushes to the surface. One thing that the mountains of Madison County

Grandpa and me

have in great abundance is cold-water springs that feed the small branches and then bigger streams! We do take advantage of our resources.

My grandfather designed a wooden trough, about seven feet long by sixteen inches wide by eight inches deep that we keep in the spring drain. He cut a notch in the top of both ends to let the cold water flow through. We use old half-gallon or gallon sized lard buckets made of metal with good tight lids to store milk and other food needing to stay cold. We sink them about six or seven inches in the cold water in that drain-box and place a flat rock on top to keep things from floating out or turning over. We stack thick flat rocks to build a shelf from the bottom of the box to cool the meat, butter and other items that we do not want to get wet. There is one problem with our spring, however. It comes out of a crack in a rock at the base of a mountain across the creek from our house. In order to fetch our drinking water, or milk or anything else stored there, we must walk a foot log over the creek.

On the other side of my family, Grandpa Moses Reese is an academic who attended Mars Hill College and did surveying and taught school. Grandma Reese is the boss of their household. Grandpa is a good surveyor, and Boyce Lumber Company offers him a job to survey a big timber spread in Tennessee. He would have to stay there and come home on the weekends until he gets that surveyed out, a good paying job, but she will not let him go. "No sir, you'll not spend time from here at night."

But she cannot get him to work where she needs him in the field. The family goes to work the field to work and he takes his paper or a magazine and sits down in the shade and reads. He walks to the store at Joe probably three miles and gets the mail every few days, gets the paper, maybe gets a magazine he's ordered. On the way back home he sits down on the bank and goes to sleep.

He is slow and deliberate. One particular time my other grandpa, Grandpa Plemmons, my mother's daddy, makes me mad. I am helping him cut tobacco and he says, "Come on son, speed it up a little bit."

I say, "I'm cutting fast enough."

He says, "Aw, you're as slow as Moses Reese."

I say, "You don't talk about my people that way." Even so, I love my Grandpa Plemmons since he is more like a daddy to me since my daddy is gone so much.

While the vast majority of people in Madison are primarily farmers, the Reeses of Madison County are mostly academics like my grandfather. My dad, being a medical man, makes it very clear that he cannot deliver babies with the rough hands of a farmer. I don't know what his five brothers use for an excuse.

All my dad's family was raised at the head of Long Branch, just to the right of Poplar Gap where the old home place is, turn above it, come over Little Creek, last house. There's Buckeye hanging right over top of it at Max Patch. When they get older and out of there, all of his family gets some education. Uncle Verlon will work as an agriculture inspector for the state and Uncle Roy as a federal ATU revenue agent, Alcohol Tobacco Unit, commonly known as a revenuer. Normally my people do not want any level of government interfering in their affairs, unless like in his case, it's their jobs.

Uncle Roy knows all the local bootleggers. Thing about it is, he has a way with him that is respected by everyone who has an eye to distinguish between the agents that are unfair and unduly cruel and those that are okay. Uncle Roy is the type that if he knows the person growing up, has a relationship with them, when he catches them at the still, he does not take them into jail. He says, "I'm going to cite you, but first you've got to stay here and get your crops in, so your family can eat. Get your family ready because you might have to serve time in prison. I want to speak at the trial on your behalf." They know him this way and not as an enemy. He is the glue that later holds the family together after my grandmother becomes bedfast.

She is the glue that holds it together as I am growing up.

The year is 1935 — Dad comes home from medical school. This is the first time I can remember ever seeing my Dad. We move about eight miles down the road to Bluff, a little settlement at the base of Bluff Mountain, at the northern end of the Spring Creek Flats. Our house is a small, three roomed, green trimmed house near the village post office-store combination.

The year is 1936 — Dad takes me with him to a neighbor's house about a mile distance who has a battery radio, and we listen to the Joe Louis and Max Schmeling fight. It is a short fight. Joe knocks Max out in the first round, and it sure is a long walk home! Dad carries me part of the way.

1937 and I am about seven years old — My Grandpa Plemmons begins teaching me to fish on Meadow Fork Creek with a cane pole and a worm, fishing for what people around here call Shasta trout. These Shasta rainbows were brought in from a tributary of the McCloud River in California's Cascade Mountain Range in the late nineteenth century. The continental railroad had been completed a few years before, opening the possibility of transporting fish by rail. The agents packed the eggs in wet moss they had gathered along the streams, shipped them to the hatchery in the east, where they were raised until the hatchery could stock the streams, including those here in the Spring Creek area. Hatchery supported trout fishing extends from Bluff through the flats of Spring Creek to the intersection at the Doggettt Mountain Road.

Meadow Fork at Keenerville Schoolhouse

From Grandpa Plemmons I learn the foundations of fishing. That the headwaters of these mountain streams are where a breed of trout exist best, preferring the cool temperatures over the warmer waters downstream. That the native trout here are the brook trout, which he calls speckles. That the brown trout were brought in generations ago from Scotland, England, Germany, giving different varieties of them throughout these streams. My grandfather is an avid fisherman, but he is a worm fisherman. He fishes Cataloochee and Big Creek over on the other side of the mountains, the streams flowing into the Pigeon River.

Fishing with my Grandpa, I realize I will have to learn to read a creek before I can successfully fish, to know where the fish are and to know what fish are in that particular stream. I also learn early that the browns are my favorite to both catch and eat, although the rainbows are the most spectacular because they jump. Once in a while browns will jump, but I think it is because of the water pressure that changes from surface to stream bed. Most of the time browns prefer the bottom, making them harder to catch. A rainbow gets out in the trout water and feeds, but old brown, he will lay back beside where this waterfall is cascading off and whirling, stirring the water so that it brings the food back to him. The speckles are the easiest to catch even though they are up in the upper ends of the creeks, where the bushes are closing in. But they feed vigorously.

1939 — In late fall and winter all men and boys hunt and trap for meat and money. I get my first gun when I am nine years old. It is a Remington bolt action repeater, twenty-two caliber. My Dad gets it as pay for delivering a baby instead of his usual fee of thirty-five dollars. We eat a lot of squirrel meat in the fall after that. Since it is hard to get shells, and many times I only have four or five bullets, I only try for head-shots. I have to become a good shot!

The grown men hate to see this little boy coming to the Turkey-shoots at Thanksgiving and Christmas!

Sometime in the forties — My mother was a farm girl growing up and likes living on a farm so much she insists that we three children do, too. With my father being away again so much in school and working in hospitals in Johns Hopkins or White Plains or Massachusetts General, she persuades him to buy a small farm.

Dad buys the Miller farm. It is a great place! It has forty-nine acres, about one-third in woodland, ten acres in pasture, and the rest in farmland. There's a two story house and out-buildings, all built with sawmill type lumber on the outside, rough and unpainted. The main house with four rooms downstairs and two up is sealed on the inside with four inch tongued and grooved ceiling boards. It also has a front and back porch.

The house is heated with wood through a cook-stove in the kitchen and a fireplace in the living room. It is my job to get up first in the mornings and build the fires in the cookstove and fire-place. In the winter time I wear long-handle underwear and do not put on any other clothing until the fires are going good. One winter morning, after a big snow storm the night before, I get up to build the fires and look outside to see a rabbit in the far end of the chicken lot. I grab my twenty-two rifle and step out into about ten inches of snow, barefooted, and I shoot that rabbit in the head. I run from the house, up through the gate and down into the lower end of the lot to get that fresh meat wearing nothing except long-handles!

In the winter time I spend most of the time each day getting wood when I'm not at school. The chestnut blight is at its peak and the dead chestnut poles are dry and solid, the best wood for getting a good fire started. They burn very hot for heating that cookstove oven and also, make the best tasting biscuits!

On the other hand, hickory and white oak are best for the fire-place. They burn hotter and last longer. I take my mule and we log all kinds of wood. In order for me to stay warm outside in those sub-zero winters, my wardrobe consisted of two pairs of long-handles, two pairs of overalls, a pair of high-topped boots with artic galoshes to keep them dry, thick wool socks, thick lumberman type shirts, gloves, and a heavy coat.

The farm also has a good, three-stall, two story barn, a large chicken house and lot, a crib and feed storage combination, a smoke house for the hog meat, and most important of all for a ten year old boy and a twelve year old girl, a great creek running just through the back yard with a high waterfall about fifty yards up the creek! My sister, Cleo, and I learn to swim in the creek water behind the house where there are deep pools cut by the waterfall. We can start at the top and slide from one pool to the next one below. It is a favorite meeting place for the young people on Sunday afternoons.

That's me riding a homemade wagon down a major thoroughfare, Bluff Mountain Road, and our closest neighbor, Charles Henderson watching. I use gears from an old cotton mill for the wheels and later install a steering wheel.

Our house is also the place the young people meet on Saturday nights to play games and listen to the Grand Ole Opry. It also gives the preacher fodder for his sermon the next day, sometimes! Our house is about the only place in the community where we can meet, except for the church meetings.

One of the main entertainments while living on a farm in Bluff is for us boys to get together after church on Sundays and ride horses (I have a mule) on the Appalachian Trail. That, and riding an old put-together cart. I always want a bicycle, though.

Daddy comes on leave one day and my mother tells him I have been smoking out in the barn. Her concern is that I will set the barn on fire.

Just so happens our cow is pregnant and my father comes up with a suggestion to get me to quit.

"If you stop smoking and if the calf is a male, then you can raise it and sell it and have the money to buy a bicycle. If it is a female, then we'll have to keep it for our own milk cow."

I do get my bicycle. It is the first store bought bicycle in the whole community, an *Elgin* I order from the *Sears and Roebuck* catalog. I soon find riding on the rocky Bluff Mountain Road requires me to become an expert at balancing.

I usually tag around after boys who are older than me, the big boys. There is one that is always playing tricks on me, Warren. I often spend the night at his house and even though we are not kin, I call his mother Aunt Lelia. That is just a respect. We call the old people Uncle this, Aunt this. That's the way it is.

This one particular morning we are doing Warren's chores. His family has a farm with a lot of land and a big team of Clydesdale horses. There's a shop for fixing plows, actually a blacksmith shop with everything fancy, as fancy goes in these days. They even have a corn mill that uses a gasoline engine. That is my friend's job on Saturdays, to run that corn mill. It has a huge tank with a lid and a spout and runs by cranking a handle. We go in the mill and I follow him around and around until he finally says, "JB, lift that lid and look down in there and tell me what you see." I raise that lid and look in. He cranks that oil right on my face. I say, "I'm going to tell Aunt Lelia on you." He gets out some soap, and you talk about washing a fellow's head, not that I don't need it.

Ern, his younger brother, plays a good trick on me once, too. He tells my mama at church to send me to their place where they had some of these "special apples," sweet apples that ripen fairly early. So she sends me to get the apples and Ern is there alone at the farmhouse. I tell him, "Ern, I come up to get some of those sweet apples. Where's that apple tree?" I am a slow learner to catch on to some of this stuff, but he tells me it is way up at the other end of the bald. Gosh, they own acres and acres right under the Bluff Mountain, this big, gently-sloping real estate. It is good laying land, easy to get over, rich land, but a tad rocky. They had stacked field rocks, making a rock fence I have to climb over every so often to get there. There are apple trees everywhere. Of course everyone has apple trees.

He tells me the exact rock fence where that tree with the "special apples" is and I head off, alone. I know what these apples look like, and that's what I'm searching for, but I walk for a long time and still can't find the tree. I go back to their house. "Ern, I couldn't find that apple tree. There wasn't no apple tree around there where you told me."

Aunt Lelia is home by now and she asks me, "Where'd he tell you that apple tree was?" I tell her. She says, "Ern, you come here, old buddy." She goes out and cuts her a hickory switch. She whips him right there. I don't mind seeing him get a whipping. They are a mischievous lot, and she doesn't put up with that.

Tricks are another form of entertainment. Grown people play them, but young people are bad to pull tricks on even younger kids. And the younger kids get mad and then fight back.

August 1940 — It's in the middle of the night when Mama wakes us to get everyone out of the house. Unbeknownst to us, a huge hurricane is approaching and the great flood of 1940 is forcing us to flee. The little branch beside our house is up four or five feet above its banks, to the

My mother, Nola Plemmons Reese

porch and about to wash the house away! It is still pouring the rain and Mama wraps a quilt around each of us and takes us out the back door and up the hill to the garden. From there we go through a barbed wire fence, a real chore getting through with those quilts on! Mama is carrying my younger brother David and those quilts keep hanging up on the barbs. We run

51

down a road bank, then through another fence on the other side of the road to Vance Russell's house on a ridge. He owns the store and post office and has been hollering for us to get out. The rain finally subsides and the house is saved, with some water damage.

Back in the time somewhere in or around 1941 — Moonshining and sawmills are the most frequently found industries in the county and only one of them is legal! Burley tobacco and Stokely Beans are the cash crops for farmers in the flats. Maybe this is where one saying unique to our mountain region comes from, "I got behind a bean truck," when we're explaining why we're late.

My money making activity in the summer is picking Stokely beans for local farmers. The wage is ten cents per hour or twelve cents per bushel. The average wage for a grown man for a ten hour day is one dollar. However, small boys and girls can pick as much or more than grown people since they are closer to the ground and do not have to bend so far. When the beans are the right size they have to be picked in a hurry, so the pickers live with the farmer until the picking is complete. Room and meals are free. I live with the Brian Plemmons family for seven days and make seven dollars. Also, I gather herbs to sell, such as Dock-root, Poke-root, Mullein, or Sassafras bark. Every herb has to be dried thoroughly before the buyer will take it!

1944 — By the time I am fourteen, I am running a trap line for mink and muskrats, and hunting at night for possums and skunks with my best dog, Rex. A number one muskrat pelt fetches three dollars. A mink brings seventeen to twenty-five, depending on how big and black it is, a big possum, fifty cents and a nearly black skunk, a dollar and a half, although it is almost impossible to catch a skunk without getting the scent on me! The dog always catches and kills the skunk on the ground, but really stirs things up and gets sick and that ends night hunts.

I put the skunk in my tow sack, take it home and skin it the next day after school along with anything else I catch in my traps. The skunk scent is very difficult to get off the skin and sometimes it will still be on when I get to school! The teacher grabs her nose and points me toward the principal's office. He grabs his nose and points me toward the road home! It is a three mile walk, and suits me just fine! Besides, at this point, the only thing I like about school is playing catcher on the baseball team.

Irish potatoes grow especially well in the black soil of Madison. However, they do not grow as well in east Tennessee, so I plant an extra half acre to sell in Newport or Greenville, Tennessee. Number one grade will bring three dollars per bushel.

1943-46, wartime — Dad joins the US Navy and is away from home again. Gas is rationed during the war and it is not unusual NOT to see a car on the road all day long, especially on a Saturday afternoon when some of us young teenagers manage to get loose from work and get a dollar from somewhere in our overalls. We walk the miles to Hot Springs to see the movie featuring, usually Hopalong Cassidy or Bob Steele. It is eight miles from Bluff and an additional five from Spring Creek, just a normal walk in these days. There will be eight to twelve of us walking during these trips, and there are usually a few fist fights and trick playing by the older boys on the younger ones. This usually results in a rock throwing contest, especially at the Van Cliffs that seem to defy gravity as we look straight down to the creek a thousand or so feet below. A few of us, maybe only one or two of our best baseball pitchers, can throw a rock to the creek.

There is one particular boy is that is overbearing and loves to pick on younger kids. I become his favorite target. He is the catcher on the baseball team and he is good at dodging

53

rocks. A person has to be good to hit that rascal. I throw enough rocks at him to load a dump truck.

We move to Hendersonville during the war when my mother gets a job working in a factory making parachutes and I get a newspaper delivery route. I attend a Boy Scout meeting. The lesson that day is on boxing and they use me as a guinea pig. This guy is sort of known for his fisticuffs. They put the gloves on me and gather around and kind of juice me up, "Hey, you, mountain boy here, this boy, don't hurt him." I fall for it. They put the boxing gloves on him, but I have had more experience than him. When this thing is over they are going to get me, the whole bunch of them, these Boy Scouts. I back up…I am used to defending myself throwing rocks at the Bluff, so I look for some rocks. There are a lot of big cinders from the nearby cotton mill, and I get me a huge cinder in both hands. I lay one on the front fellow and I slow them down. I keep backing up, picking up more cinders. I am pretty accurate with them. I never go to another Boy Scout meeting.

Back in the time, early September, 1947 — I am in the eleventh grade in Spring Creek High School and an unhappy seventeen-year-old rebel, getting into more trouble than necessary, and needing some strong discipline! Dad is too busy with his night and day medical practice to do the job, but, having just gotten out of the military, he knows who and what could give the discipline I need, and then some. I fall right into the trap. I had been thinking about quitting that boring school and getting out of that backward environment. So one day in

My eleventh grade school picture, sixteen years old

early September I ask him if he will sign my permission application to join the United States Army Airforce. He agrees on the condition that I finish high school in service, well, that and the condition that he can get Mom to sign the application also. She is very reluctant to see her boy leave at first, but, after Dad reminds her how much more pleasant it will be around the house without teachers and principals asking for help with me, she agrees. She cries a little when I leave. I tell some people that it is likely because of sadness, but it could have been mixed with joy!

September 18, 1947 — I am sworn into the Air Force in Columbia, South Carolina and loaded onto a C-47 and flown to Lackland Air Force base, San Antonio, Texas for sixteen weeks basic training. It doesn't take but a very few days to realize what a great mistake I have made! That big red faced Texas drill sergeant will get his the moment they put a gun in my hands. Little do I know that in three years that I will be doing the same job for new recruits that he is now doing to and for me. I go through basic training for thirteen weeks but when my father becomes sick, I come home on emergency leave. By the time I return, my outfit has moved on and I have to join another outfit to finish basic training. Because of all that, I am the only one in my original outfit that didn't make PFC.

I move to a new assignment at Walker Air Force Base in Roswell, New Mexico about the time of the alien event. Nobody much believes them. It is investigated and investigated and the Air Force is continually saying it is weather balloons people see, until after a while, some of the military comes out and give more facts about the little man that they found and took to the undertaker's there in Roswell.

1950 — My three year enlistment will be up in September, but the Korean War starts in June and I am extended. I wind up doing three more years until the war is over.

1952 and I am stationed with the 98th Bomb Wing in Japan, flying on B-29's refueling F-82's, F-84's, and finally F-86 jet aircraft over Korea.

At Yokota Air Base in Japan

1953 — Few people are believers about the incident in Roswell, New Mexico, unless they actually experience it, and I happen to be one of them that actually experience it with four other people at the same time.

I arrive back from deployment in Korea. When I had gone over, one of the sergeants I was with had left a car in San Francisco since that is where we shipped out. Now we are going to be stationed together at Forbes Air Force Base in Kansas, so when we return from Korea and land in British Columbia, Canada we plan to drive together across country. We go to the Air Force base in Seattle, Washington to get paid, and of course, my records are lost. There are four other guys with me including Sergeant Cline who owns the car. Instead of being delayed there, one of them calls home and asks his family if they would lend me the money and I will pay them back. They say "yes" because they do not want him to be delayed just because my money has not yet come. So we catch a bus, come down to San Francisco to get the car planning to ride together to Dallas, Texas. I am riding that far with them and catching the bus on home.

Important to the story, the railroad tracks follow the roads in that part of the country through New Mexico and Texas. So we are riding along, probably three o'clock in the morning and taking turns driving. I am sitting in the back seat with two others, about half asleep. Somebody says, "Where's that train?"

Sergeant Cline is driving his car at that time. He answers, "I guess it would be over there on that railroad track. Where else would you expect a train to be?" It is not unusual to see a train coming, to meet one, to cross one since we were on a regular road, in central Texas with tumbleweeds and semi-desert on both sides. He looks out the window. "My God, look, look, look," and he runs the car off the road into the tumbleweeds.

He stops. I look out the window and I see it too. We jump out. We don't know what it might do. All of us run around behind the car looking over our shoulders at that thing. It is sitting there wobbling, hovering about fifty to seventy-five feet off the ground. Huge. Big. B-29's that we had been flying in Korea have a wing span of a hundred and forty-three feet. This thing in front of us has a diameter on it that is almost that big. I see why this is called a flying saucer because the top is like a cup turned upside down on its saucer.

All around the edges are lights similar to torches showing different colors, like when a blow torch changes from orange to red to blue. It appears to be made of aluminum, about the same color as an unpainted airplane and I cannot see any windows or doors. We can see it well because the moon is shining and there is some light reflecting off the object's propulsion system.

It sounds like a train, which is why we wonder if it is a diesel engine. We probably watch it two or three minutes, but when that thing flies off, it goes fast, so fast, if I hadn't had my eyes on it, I don't believe I could have picked it up.

We know we have never seen anything like it before. Of course we have been hearing about flying UFO's reported by responsible people, but we are still just in a state of shock. We start describing what we had seen to each other, and all of us have seen exactly the same thing.

Then we start thinking.

Here we are, all of us on leave, going home. We've got fifteen, thirty days, whatever they gave us. We discuss the possibility of reporting it. No. We report this, then the authorities will send us to a psycho lab. No, we're not going to report this.

It is getting along towards breakfast time when we stop in a little town further down the road. There is a café and we stop to eat. The one of our bunch who is always the clown decides to speak about it. This waitress takes our order and when she come back he says, "What would you say if I told you we saw a flying saucer earlier today?"

She says, "I'd say you were crazy."

"That's what I thought you'd say."

We put a cap on it and never mention it again. Our main objective is to go home.

When I do get home, I tell my mama and she says, "You've been to war. You're just nervous."

I tell my dad. My dad, whether he believes it exists or not, he believes that I believe. He says, "As far as you're concerned, you saw it."

I go over to the store my grandpa is running near Lenoir and I know pretty much what he is going to say. I tell him the story and ask, "What do you think of that, Grandpa?"

He says, "Shit," and spits on the hot wood stove. It sizzles, like it is as disgusted at my story as he is.

Home with my father and my first cousin, Arliss Suttles

September, 1953 through 1990 — I am discharged from the Air Force and come home to Lenoir, North Carolina where my Grandpa runs a store he had purchased in 1953. I meet my future wife, Helen Whisnant, in October of that year. I enter Lenoir Rhyne College in Hickory, North Carolina on the GI Bill in 1954, and get married July 10, 1954. Our first son John is born in 1955. I graduate Lenoir Rhyne in August of 1957, and we move to St Petersburg, Florida where I teach two years at Tyrone Junior High. My second son Brian is born in 1958. I then return to Lenoir in June, 1959 to teach world history under an assistantship and I earn an MA at Appalachian State in 1960. I go back to the same school in Florida for two years and then back to Lenoir where our third son, Scott is born in 1962. I teach at Kings Creek High School 1962-1963 and serve as principal at Patterson School for Boys 1964-1967. Our fourth son, Eric is born in 1967. I become principal at Collettsville Elementary 1968-1970. I teach at Hudson High School and eventually at South Caldwell High School until my final year of teaching in mathematics and US history in 1989-1990.

1990 — I retire in June and after that my friend Newland Saunders and I fish or grouse hunt on Tuesdays and Thursdays, depending on the season. We fish all the local trout streams in Wilkes and Watauga Counties. We travel and camp and fish the streams of the Smoky Mountains and the lakes and streams of the Little Tennessee River drainage. We also fish in Montana, Alaska, and Canada.

Fishing in Alaska

Chapter Five
A Mountain Education:
My Community's Story

Back in the year 1919 — There is a two story school containing four classrooms—two for the high school and two for the younger students. It is known locally as the Gap of the Mountain School, also once known as Spring Creek Seminary, but now officially known as Spring Creek School, Madison County, North Carolina.

Bonnie Woody, the principal as well as the English, math, history, Latin and spelling teacher all in one, is filling in the required end of the year forms, only this day is March 31, 1919, earlier than usual. She enters the data, not at all conceiving the thought that nearly a hundred years later, a researcher going through dusty boxes of files in the state archives would uncover this very end-of-year report.

Thirty-two students in the high school, grades eight through ten, she writes. None promoted. She pencils in the zero in its appropriate slot. She reports on the grammar grades as well, two additional teachers, both women. Between the three of them, the total student population they serve at Spring Creek comes to one hundred fifty-two students covering classes from first through tenth grade. Total promotions, zero.

Gap of the Mountain School children, photo courtesy of Spring Creek Community Center

Nothing seems amiss. The structure of the framed, plank building she lists as sound, although the heating and ventilation, unsatisfactory. With no electricity as yet in the valley, the heat is a wood stove and the light is natural, solar, rarely supplemented with lanterns. Tall windows allow light to filter in and heat to seep out.

Under the section labeled dormitories owned by school she pencils the word "none," yet on the line for number of boarding students enrolled, she lists five girls.

There are shade trees outside, but no bushes, shrubs or flowers. The ground soil is clay. There is not a separate room for her as principal to meet with children or parents. There are no individual student records kept. There is no library, no dictionary in the entire school, and no cafeteria. Children pack lunches in empty lard buckets. Bathrooms are outdoor privies. Desks for the students are single seaters, bolted to the floor.

The forms give her one last chance to explain the zero students promoted. Section VIII. General Remarks. Note, it says, "On this page give any pertinent facts not specifically called for elsewhere, and report any significant achievement or progress since the last annual report was made." There in thick pencil script is the explanation: "Average attendance is very low because of an epidemic raging in the community since October. Because of epidemic, school was closed before term was completed."

The details she omits. The specific epidemic she leaves out, although newspaper articles, both local and nationwide, report widespread influenza. Teachers sick and unable to find a healthy substitute, she neglects to mention, either on purpose, or because she is perhaps too sick herself to go beyond the bare necessities of reporting. Children dying? Only the churchyard stones report that. Surviving children cannot progress to the next grade level when school does not function. No one graduates that year.

1920 — The school rebounds with thirty-two students again enrolled in the upper level, but one hundred four in the two elementary classrooms. Five students board in nearby homes in order to attend the school. A new principal appears, Vealey Humphries, teaching the social studies, literature and language subjects. Ella Duncan assists part time in the high school with the math and science classes. Two additional teachers divide grades one through seven students between them into a class load of over fifty students each. By the end of the year, one student completes grade ten and graduates, and of the thirty-one others enrolled in the high school, thirteen are promoted.

1921 and another teacher begins as principal, Joe Q. Tilson. With no part time teacher, he teaches the entire high school course of study. A third teacher joins the faculty to lighten the class size of the grammar grades to less than forty children per class. Total enrollment has risen to one hundred thirty-six, with twenty-five of them in the high school. Mr. Tilson reports no separate room for a library, but eight fiction books available for students. He adds there is unsatisfactory heating and ventilation, and insufficient lighting.

The daily routine begins at 8:40 each morning in the assembly hall with an all-student chapel for the first twenty minutes. Dismissal is at four o'clock. An hour lunch break divides the day into two halves, and two twenty minute recesses offer more breaks to the students in the morning and afternoon. In his end of year report, Principal Tilson lists a playground as the greatest need of the school.

This school year lasts only twenty-nine weeks and the five students who complete the tenth grade are considered graduates, including my father. For his grammar grades, he had attended a neighborhood school, but during his high school years he must attend school several miles away. Because my grandparent's home is on Long Branch across Caldwell Mountain from Meadow Fork and Spring Creek, walking to school daily becomes an impossibility and he boards with a widow in the community, Mrs. Hunter, who needs help keeping up her farm chores. She is quite a dignified lady, soft spoken and a special kind of person who commands a great deal of respect. It is one of the few places where my father behaves himself as he is growing up! She maintains her support of him throughout my father's life, and years later, is the neighbor who keeps his penicillin supplies in her gas powered refrigerator.

1922 — The school population increases to one hundred fifty, with twenty-seven students enrolled in high school classes. On the end-of-year forms, Principal G.C. Brown reports the ages of the high school students include one twenty-two year old, one twenty-one year old, three twenty year olds, two nineteen year olds and seventeen students between the ages of fourteen and seventeen. While he teachers the entire course of study for the high school, three men and one woman teach grades one through seven. For his nine years of experience Mr. Brown is paid an annual salary of nine hundred sixty-eight dollars.

School begins with chapel exercises at 8:30, breaks for an hour at lunch at noon, and continues until four o'clock with a ten minute recess in the morning. With no tenth grade students enrolled for the year, there are no graduates in 1923.

1923 and in this academic year, only twelve students are enrolled in the high school, all listed as in their second year, or ninth grade. The total school population increases to one hundred forty-five. The older, above eighteen year olds from the year before are no longer attending school. Once again there are no graduates. Once again the principal lists the condition of the school as unsatisfactory.

Discipline is harsh and necessary both in school and at home. The independent zeal required by a man and his wife to pack up their meager belongings, leave their place of residence, come into the mountains to build a livable cabin and carve a farm out of the woods demands strict discipline out of each family member in order to survive. These people and their offspring are tough and ready to prove it. Punishment is fast and physical in most cases, as that handed down from one generation to another. The big difference between punishment at school and home is the instrument used to administer corporeal punishment. Teachers and principals' primary weapon is similar to a baseball bat with one end flattened out into a paddle. Few if any use a paddle at home. Mothers use the flat of the hand to spank the small children and a hickory switch as they get older. Fathers do not whip often until their children are in their teens.

A mountain farmer needs order and labor, and he produces both with the help of his wife. There is one basic rule taught mountain children from the beginning: Do not disrespect or sass parents or teachers or any authority in any way, place or time. To do so might get an immediate slap in the face! An older boy may get a fist to his jaw! Selective passages from the Bible are used to justify behavior. "Spare the rod and spoil the child," and "Be fruitful and multiply." Of course there are abuses, but child and adolescent psychology have not been heard of yet in these mountains. Parents and teachers feel God has given all his creatures the necessary instincts to discipline and protect their offspring. Parents who demand good discipline are respected and loved more by their children as they grow up and mature than those who pet, permit and excuse.

1924 — The Madison County School Board authorizes the patrons in Bluff to run a partition through their schoolhouse, thus making two rooms of the house. They are also instructed to cut a door in the lower side of the house.

1926 — W. C. Ingle and a delegation of interested citizens go before the Madison County School Board asking for a new building for Little Creek School. The board puts aside $1,500 in the budget subject to approval of the county's Board of Commissioners.

1928 — Certified teacher, Emma Logan, maintains a school in the Bluff community for the first, second and third graders. Classes are held in her home, making this a true schoolhouse. My family later rents one of her houses near the schoolhouse.

The county school board in Marshall has heard the plea for better schools. At their February sixth regular session, the Board of Education votes a $30,000 loan to build a new school building in Spring Creek. The County Commissioners approve.

Meanwhile, the school board orders a special election in Township Number 8 to ascertain the wishes of the community on a proposed levy of thirty cents on the one hundred dollar tax valuation on all property. These monies will be used to maintain a six month school term and to consolidate the Woody Schoolhouse in Luck, Friezeland School in Trust, Zion School in Bluff, and Spring Creek School (once known as Gap of the Mountain School and also Spring Creek Seminary).

Friezeland Students, photo courtesy of Spring Creek Community Center

Woody School photo courtesy of Spring Creek Community Center

January 1, 1929 — The Madison County School Board members meet at Spring Creek to walk through proposed locations for the school, although no decision is made at this time. Finding a five acre site required for the facility on the flats of Spring Creek presents the first hurdle. Water from the surrounding mountains funnels directly into the flatland and the proposed site of the school. During times of heavy rains, water overruns the creek banks, floods the area, and the land becomes a marsh.

Plans for the new facility in the Spring Creek community are completed and construction can begin once the final decision on the exact location for the school is made. At their February fourth meeting the board approves the purchase of land in the center of the flats belonging to Lon Ferguson at a cost of $756.56, and the adjacent land of W. H. Hipps to be used for the playground for $1,656.56. The school building will face the newly constructed Highway #209.

J.J. Baldwin of Asheville and Greenville, South Carolina is selected as the architect and he designs a rock masonry building fitting naturally into the picturesque mountains behind it. Nearby farmer John Woody along with other farmers in the area donate the many unwanted rocks from their fields for the exterior facing. Sand from Spring Creek is used for the mortar. Mr. Woody also provides much of the water needed during construction. Other easily accessible materials are used throughout the school. With an overabundance of wood available in nearby forests, and a plentiful supply of well-trained loggers in the community, interior framing and floors are built with chestnut, pine, and oak from the local sawmills.

In a cost-cutting decision, sheetrock is chosen for the overhead walls rather than plaster, and although electricity is not available, a contract is awarded to the lowest bidder to wire the building. Anticipating frequent flooding, architect Baldwin elevates the school's floor high above the water line and the front entrance requires several additional steps. The furnace remains located in flood level beneath the school.

The board approves a $5,404.05 payment on July first to Jerry Liner for construction, along with a later $2,500.00 payment and another $500 payment for waterproofing the basement. With no electrical power, manpower accomplishes the construction. Even with all the innovations, a cafeteria is not a part of the original construction. When construction is completed, the eleven classrooms and gymnasium facility is valued at $45,000.

The community volunteers to help in several more ways by spreading shale to make driveways around the building and grading the baseball diamond on the playground. Local school committees are responsible for overseeing the daily affairs. Those members appointed for Spring Creek are Homer Reeves, Dave Ferguson, John Gardener and A. N. Woody.

The youngest children in the Little Creek, Roaring Fork, Meadow Fork, Keenerville and Poplar Gap districts are to remain in their currently assigned schools, although seventh graders and beyond from those school districts will now attend Spring Creek.

A recent view of abandoned Keenerville School

Meadow Fork School students from the files of Ruby Kent,
photo courtesy of Spring Creek Community Center

Poplar Gap School photo courtesy of Major Jean Frese

September 5, 1929, the Madison County Board of Education holds a called meeting to walk through and accept the new school building. They hire a janitor, Mr. Eulas Ledford, and offer a salary of forty dollars per month. Two bus routes are proposed to transport the students requiring the school board to purchase school trucks from a Chevrolet dealership in Madison County. School trucks, by order of the board, are not to be taken away from their regular runs until all school children are carried home. They may then be used to convey athletic teams to activities, provided the coach or other teacher appointed by the principal also rides in the truck.

School photo courtesy of Spring Creek Community Center

On the very first, first day of school, September 9, 1929 children arrive either by walking or on one of the two buses driven by Roscoe Blankenship and Paul Allison and later by N. L. Ponder and Stuart Plemmons. Eager students are greeted at opening chapel by three high school and seven grammar grade teachers, including Principal J. O. Wells who carries a full teaching load in the high school English classes along with his administrative duties. The high school now consists of eighth through eleventh grades. The addition of the eleventh grade requirement for graduation brings back seven students who would have graduated the year before. Through the consolidation of these nearest small schools, the Spring Creek School's first student population totals three hundred and thirty pupils.

Differences between this new facility and their one to four room schools begin with a separate room for a library that houses three hundred and twenty-five books, all newly purchased. Another separate room is the science laboratory with limited equipment for the study of biology, general science, and physical geography. The latest Rand McNally maps are found in each classroom. With no cafeteria, children continue to pack lunches from home. Heat is no longer from a wood stove, but from steam produced by a coal furnace kept operating by janitor Eulas Ledford. The assembly hall can be adapted to a gymnasium, and basketball now becomes a popular form of recreation. (Go Tigers!) Lighting for evening games comes from carbide lamps that illuminate the gymnasium, but nothing else. At a Saturday night game on January 26, 1930 against Marshall High School, the Spring Creek girls defeat Marshall 16-15, while the boys lose 14-7.

Zion School building and property in Bluff is sold to T. C. Finley for $100.00, payable with one third down, one third in six months and one third within twelve months.

School Superintendent C. M. Blankenship announces a free Teacher Training School for the benefit of teachers having Elementary B certificates and high school graduates that cannot attend college yet want to begin a career in education. Those completing the course will be issued an Elementary A certificate.

1930 — Graduation day, April 25th when the first ever graduates of Spring Creek School, Annie Davis, Rickman Davis, Bertha Hunter, Ada Meadows, William Meadows and Alma Phoenix are celebrated in the multipurpose assembly hall/gymnasium. Each of them completed at least sixteen units of credit for graduation. In his end of year report general remarks, Principal Wells writes, "First year school has been organized. We think we met requirements for a standard school and desire to be put on the accredited list."

Fall 1931 — The Logan School in Bluff closes when Mrs. Logan begins teaching at Spring Creek School. Her entire annual salary, $792.00 is based on her A level certification, her five years of experience at the Logan School and her education at Marquette College.

1931 — Campus beautification projects begin with the land being leveled and grass sown during the short growing season. A hickory tree is planted.

It is not unusual in winter to have subzero temperatures on top of snow and ice for days at a time. School is never cancelled. The snow chains are rarely taken off the rear wheels of the school buses from the first snow in November to spring thaw in March or April. The school buses to Spring Creek High only run on Highway #209 and Meadow Fork Road (when it runs at all). Many high school students walk several miles from Long Branch and Little Creek to catch the bus on Meadow Fork Road. Walking to the school or the bus in early mornings causes our hair to develop a layer of frost.

The back of the school, photo courtesy of Spring Creek Community Center

The main obstacle to daily school attendance beyond the harsh winter weather and unpaved roads is a lack of value placed on education by parents in many cases. A few think education is the work of the devil. To compound the issue, approximately ninety percent of the people depend on steep-country small farms for survival and a significant amount of them place much more importance on keeping children home from school to work the farm. Human labor at home is a much higher priority than education for the children that are old enough to work. Although state law requires compulsory education to age 16, it also permits parents to hold their children away from school to work the family farms.

Many of these isolated back country communities like Popular Gap and Keenerville have a church building which doubles as an elementary school for the youngest children during the week. Sometimes the teacher in the isolated church schools have no more than a high school diploma themselves. Despite this, education in these combo church schools prove to be an effective ungraded system. Children in each grade know what the next higher grade is doing. The more motivated and more capable students frequently skip years and move up grades.

1933 — Sixth grade teacher Edith Ferguson steps in as the girls' advisor at the school, although she does not teach in the high school. For several years, there have been boys and girls Glee Clubs. This year adds a literary society and a 4-H club.

The political climate in Madison has an effect on education during the Great Depression. In the thirties and forties for the most part, neither Republican nor Democrats pay much attention to who is running for jobs in Washington. Rather, the political emphasis is local officers and who goes to Raleigh. Politically, Madison has always been a swing county, and consequently, there is an intense game fought fiercely between friends and foe alike during political campaigns, depending on one's political persuasion. "To the winners go the spoils..." and the jobs. This includes educators. There is no such thing as tenure, and the political party in power determines who gets the jobs from county superintendent to teachers, to janitors, to school bus drivers and anyone else who is involved in education. Everyone is hired for one year at a time. Rules may be made in Raleigh and Washington, but they are enforced in Madison by Madison. It is a common rumor that teachers who live and vote in Madison pay a campaign contribution to the party in office at the time.

1935 — In the past, the one hundred sixty day school year typically commences in August and ends in April. This year changes and starts in September after harvest and ends in early May. Class size in the elementary school at Spring Creek surges to over fifty students per teacher. Of the school's nine teachers, four hold A level certificates and five hold B levels. Third grade teacher, Mrs. Burgess, begins a music curriculum using the piano in the auditorium. There is no physical education program, but a lunch recess is supervised by the classroom teachers, and children make their own fun. For lunch, children often bring a quart jar filled with cornbread and milk, setting it on the windowsill for refrigeration. Of the four hundred students enrolled at Spring Creek this year, only two hundred thirty-nine are promoted to the next grade. Standardized tests are used as the basis for promotion, and there is no social promotion.

I am five years old and selected to be the mascot for the school's graduating class. Because my father is absent from our home attending medical school, my mother requires a great deal of assistance after the birth of my younger brother. A couple of high school seniors, twins Anabel and Annalou Caldwell, who live about a mile up the road, visit her a good bit. They mostly help mother by playing with me, and by taking me to school with them, even though I am a preschooler. This is customary when an older sibling is responsible for child care. No one thinks anything about my being there, and I soon have the run of the place.

They introduce me throughout all the school. Eventually their classmates select me as the school mascot. I even have a part in the end of the year, junior/senior play. There I am on stage and nature calls. I stop the action and announce to everyone, fellow actors as well as the audience, "I got to go pee." The crowd roars!

That's me in front of the Class of 1935

1936 — I begin my formal education at Spring Creek School. My first grade teacher is Viola Fowler, the same first grade teacher for everyone entering school. The Primer reader is a paperback series featuring the main characters Dick and Jane and their dog Spot. The hard back reader is *Play Time*. Each morning when we arrive at school, we go into our classrooms. The teachers gather their classes and take us to the gymnasium where we sit on the floor and mingle with other classes while the teachers lead us in morning devotions.

1938 — The North Carolina State Legislature votes to require twelve years of education for a high school diploma. Implementing this change is left to the local unit. Reconfiguring the local school systems takes several years before the plan is complete in Spring Creek, so for now, students continue to graduate after the eleventh grade.

1939 — Remarks from the state Associate Division of Instruction suggest, "This school appears to have made a start in equipment. No school can do the best work without it. Decide items you need most. Get the county to help." With or without county help, some improvements are made. Curtains are added to shade the windows, and a hundred foot cloak unit is built. A hectograph duplicator is used to print worksheet copies. Also known as a jellygraph, it is a shallow container filled with a treated gelatin. The first step is to make a master copy with a special transfer ink, usually in a purple color. This image is laid face down on the gelatin for the dye to soak in and form the page to be printed. Once the master copy is removed, the final step is to press individual sheets of paper on the gelatin and transfer the dye to each sheet, one at a time.

No film strip or motion picture projectors are available since without electricity in the school, both would be useless.

The largest class size is Mrs. Viola Fowler's first grade with fifty-eight students. No special education teachers are available to help struggling students. Of this year's three hundred thirty-five grammar grade students, two hundred and three are promoted.

1940 — School Committee members Mr. Ledford, Mr. Phoenix and Mr. Garner appear before the Board of Education to request a drain for the basement at Spring Creek School. In addition, they ask to erect a house for the janitor, to cost approximately two hundred dollars, for the purpose of protecting the school property and for the janitor to be available at all times.

The largest class size is Mrs. May Boone Robinson's with forty-four second grade students. By the time the year ends, in the section on the yearly report listing any improvements made since the last annual report was submitted, the exhausted principal/high school history and science teacher, Mr. J. S. Holland simply writes,

"We haven't had time as yet."

It is a typical year for the surrounding grammar grade schools that send their older students into Spring Creek High School. Roaring Fork in Joe serves the first seven grades of that community's children. The eighty-three students are split into two classes, first second and third graders in Ruby Kent's class, and originally four other grades with Lucile Roberts. When the teachers plead for help with large class sizes, the seventh graders are sent to Spring Creek School and remaining students reassigned.

To the west of Spring Creek and further into the mountains, Keenerville School teacher Hazel Angel Fleming herds her twenty-two students covering first through six grades into one room. There are no maps and globes, no classroom equipment beyond recitation chairs and student desks. Drinking water comes from a nearby spring. The bathrooms, like in these other small outlying schools, are outdoor pit facilities.

Further along yet another dirt road, teacher/principal, Mrs. Novile Hawkins, joins three other women to make up the faculty of Little Creek School. The school facilities that double as a church on weekends are similar to Keenerville, although the building itself boasts four classrooms. The one request from the principal, "Please give us suggestions for starting a library." The one hundred twenty-four students are divided unevenly between the teachers, the thirty-nine first graders making up the only single grade class in the school. The others are combinations of more than one grades.

The school at Maple Springs on the Madison/Haywood County line is owned by the Salvation Army and directed by Cecil Brown. Major Brown's Mountain Mission has impacted lives throughout several communities. The classrooms are in the upstairs of the trading post.

Growing up, she saw a need for a mission to her people and a lack of what the church could be for them. Before she established her mission, circuit riding preachers ministered to the mountain people. They preached the word of God, and then went on to the next church on their circuit, not providing any mission service beyond preaching, baptizing, and funerals. Major Brown's mother for years had prayed for a preacher who would put down roots and minister to the people, but she never

Maple Springs Trading Post and School photo courtesy of Major Jean Freese

had any idea the answer to her prayer would be her own daughter. Mountain people are normally hesitant about a woman preacher, but since Cecil Brown is from here, she soon wins their hearts. She makes her rounds visiting the people on her horse named Daisy, riding the mare wherever she goes. The weather does not get too bad for her to get out and help somebody.

She builds a house to board children next door to the Maple Springs Church, Haywood House. It is not designed specifically as an orphanage, but more for children when they need to be removed from the home for various reasons.

Nearby is Max Patch School, another school on the Madison/Haywood County line.

Max Patch School photo courtesy of Lottie Mae Frisbee Gregory

Poplar Gap School is a Salvation Army Church on Sunday and a school during the week. My uncle, Gonnie Reese, my father's youngest brother, who, like the rest of our family, is a product of this kind of school, becomes a teacher there. In these years, education is set up by the leaders in the community who see the need. They look amongst themselves and pick someone to be the teacher who is just a little better educated than anybody else, or a little smarter. Often the only person available is somebody who only went through the eleventh grade of public school and has no formal teacher education.

Down the mountain from Maple Springs and Poplar Gap is the community of Joe with Meadow Fork School. Three teachers divide the ninety-six children between them. In the midst of limited books and no library, and definitely no electricity, the fifth, sixth and seventh graders form a Literary Society with their teacher, Mr. Jack V. Joyce.

Because of limited transportation to Spring Creek School, these small local schools remain open for the younger children. The older students are more able to walk across the mountains in poor weather to board the bus at the few stops it makes.

The school's culture in these times require tough educators to maintain discipline in a room full of tough students. The opportunity for abuse from a sadistic teacher a few times presents itself to become abrasive as the teacher attempts to survive these tough students. However there are mostly good teachers who use the paddle sparingly and create good learning situations. Students are taught to expect punishment again at home when they are caught violating the rules at school.

Several teachers ride the school bus every day, not necessarily to maintain discipline, but more as transportation to and from school. The seats are arranged on the bus with a double center seat running from the front to the back, like a bench down the middle where students sit back to back. Then there are two side seat benches facing inward, running from the front to the back and much preferred by the older students who throw us younger ones out to the middle bench. That's where the bigger boys sit and where the teacher's attention should be. Older students are bad to pull tricks on younger kids aboard the bus, and the younger kids get mad and fight back. The bus proves to be a place where all the malcontents get together. Children are lucky to get home a day or two at a time without having to fight somebody on that bus.

I am already sitting on the middle bench one day when a seventh grade student comes charging into the bus in a race to get a side seat! He pushes my head over, hard, on the iron trim of my seat! I come up immediately crying and fighting with the only weapon I have, my *Play Time Reader*, the only hard-backed book I have. I hit him under the left eyeball and cut a gash with the corner of it!! Blood splatters all over from his face and my head. A teacher is on the bus as usual and she reports me as the instigator to the principal the next day. He will not listen to my side at all, and to nobody else except the teacher! He gets out his paddle and beats me unmercifully! When I get home Mom is told, so she pulls my pants down and looks at my bloodshot butt and goes into a rage! Mom tries to get on the bus the next morning to go get that principal! However, the driver has orders to keep her off the bus.

My dad comes home during the summer after school was out for the year, and he and my uncle go looking for that principal. However, he has left the area and never comes back!

February, 1941 and Spring Creek principal J. S. Holland pens a formal letter to Miss Julia Wetherington of the Division of Instructional Services:

> *I have just received your letter regarding the inspection of our elementary department relative to the placing of the school on the accredited list. I am very sorry but I do not believe we can reach the requirements this year. We were so far behind to begin with. Until last year we did not have but a few supplementary books and the library was much behind too. As you may or may not know, the county commissioners do not cooperate with the schools very well in financial matters, so whatever we do in buying equipment we must raise the money by programs, etc. I will try my best to reach the requirements by next year.*

In North Carolina, one of the duties of the Grand Jury of the Superior Court is to inspect state and county owned buildings and agencies to determine the manner in which individuals in charge have carried out their duties to the state. A Grand Jury is convened in August to inspect the schools in the Madison County School System. Jurors visit each school in the county and find a few substandard situations at Spring Creek, mostly in reference to the water in the basement. The grand jury also reports the two school buses are overloaded, Bus #6 carries one hundred three children per trip and Bus # 39 carries ninety-seven children per trip.

Ever since the school was built in the lowlands of the flats, there have been issues with flooding in the basement. Years of forming a bucket brigade to bail out water have proven unsuccessful, so in a desperate attempt, the local men build a drainage ditch designed to route the water away from the school so that the furnace in the basement boiler room is not further damaged. A gasoline powered generator also in the boiler room supplies not only electricity for the lights, but also a constant hum in the background. Although the doors to the gym remain open and shed some light, the entry hall remains unlit for those people coming to school events in the evenings.

This is a year of remarkable improvements at Spring Creek School with a hundred and sixty supplemental readers added for the grammar grades. A much needed lunchroom is installed. It is small, located in the center section of the building, with only enough room for one grade to be seated at a time. Older students work there cleaning tables in exchange for payment for their lunches. Families in the community bring big sacks of potatoes or onions or tomatoes or other produce they grow and can to the lunchroom in exchange for their children eating a meal. The cafeteria ladies cook the food themselves, always a good healthy meal. Much of the lunchroom food comes from the depression year recovery program that brings food and nourishment to the children of the mountains, a lot of beans and hot dogs, corn bread or biscuits. The pork and beans are the first I have ever eaten. As a part of the nourishment program, during recess the teachers in the room mix a five gallon pot of chocolate milk and pour each child a cup.

Best news, all outstanding debts are paid off by the school. Worst news, Pearl Harbor is bombed. We are living in Bluff when the World War starts, getting all the war news on our battery powered radio.

The times are 1942 through 1945 — Across the globe World War II rages. In Spring Creek, fathers, brothers, uncles and sons join the armed services. Food shortages and rationing weaken the newly formed lunchroom, but locally grown food supplements the meals. We participate in the war efforts by purchasing war bonds. The School Board decides it is the Patriotic duty of the schools to cancel the Music Festival scheduled for March of 1943.

1943 — Although war time gas rationing limits travel, and rubber rationing limits school bus tire replacements, the length of the school term is increased from the previous years' eight months to add a ninth month. This year public school children across North Carolina now attend school a total of one hundred eighty days.

Five hundred dollars is moved from the general school account into a fund to maintain the janitor's house and a water line is extended from the school to the house. Drainage problems beneath the school continue and the school board, because of budget restraints, orders a pump installed instead of the requested drainage ditch. My grandfather, Jasper Plemmons, is paid fifteen dollars for his labor working at the school.

John Gentry begins teaching an Auto Mechanics Course for Spring Creek boys. Local School Committee members for Spring Creek are John Plemmons, Dave Ledford, and Glen Davis; At Roaring Fork, R. V. Ebbs, Harrison Brown and Hubert Pangle; At Keenerville, Jess Keener, Verge Beasley and Z. V. Beasley; At Poplar Gap, J. P. Norris, Reubin Lowe and H. H. Reese; At Meadow Fork, Tillman Reese, Grady Balding and H. M. Dixon.

The local committees at Poplar Gap and Meadow Fork Schools approach the Madison County School Board to argue against a proposed plan of consolidating the schools. They claim the move is unwise since several children will need to walk too far to attend school, and with rationing, there is no means of transportation for them.

1945 — The largest class size at Spring Creek is made up of thirty-five students taught by a fifth grade teacher holding a level "C" emergency teaching certificate with zero years of experience. Post war teacher shortages leave schools across the state with little options other than lowering professional requirements and hiring noncertified teachers to fill the void. Nonetheless, of the nine grammar grade teachers at Spring Creek Elementary School, six hold the standard "A" level certification.

At nearby Meadow Fork, the primary grade teacher has a county level class two certification, zero years of experience and thirty five pupils. The grammar grade teacher, who also serves as building principal, has thirty-one students, an "A" certificate, and one year of experience.

1946 — The place is Spring Creek High School, and although there is no flu epidemic like decades ago, there will be no graduating class of 1947.

Ever since the state of North Carolina's decision to expand free public education from eleven years to twelve, Madison County has planned for this day. First to eighth grades now become the grammar school and ninth through twelfth, the high school. Eleventh grade students at Spring Creek High School graduate in 1946. The tenth graders move up to eleventh grade, as usual, but by year's end in 1947, they are not finished. They must return to school the next year and become the class of 1948, the first class to complete twelve years. More teachers must be hired across the state to accommodate the extra grade, contributing to an even greater teacher shortage. Teachers are often hired with little training. My tenth grade principal is an ex-marine from World War II.

1948 — At Meadow Fork School, two men teachers, Jack Joyce and Caney Smith, divide the seven grades of eighty-three students between them for a class size of over forty students each. Mr. Joyce, a strict disciplinarian, leads morning devotions and then frequently quotes one of his favorite scriptures throughout each day, "Spare the rod, spoil the child." He

Children outside Meadow Fork School
photo courtesy of Lottie Mae Frisbee Gregory

instructs his students if they do not know the correct answer to a question, they are to say "Nebuchadnezzar."

Before the year is out, a third teacher is added, Emma Holt, taking the first through third grades. Meadow Fork's classification at the end of the academic year is non-accredited with the visiting committee pointing out an unusually high number of retentions. Meadow Fork has no library, no globes or maps, no lunchroom, and no indoor bathroom facilities. There is one dictionary for the entire student population. Yet when students from this school move into Spring Creek for their eighth grade year, they have the basic skills to succeed, because if they don't, they are held back.

Spring Creek's classification as of June 1, 1948 is accredited, even though, as at Meadow Fork, the committee points to an unusually high number of retentions. Principal Bernard Brigman gives a glimpse of the future in his annual end of year report: "No electricity this year. [1947-1948] Now being installed, and equipment ordered for use next year." The waiting equipment includes a motion picture projector and a lantern slide projector, and a set of fifty records purchased to accompany the one phonograph.

This summer has been unusually hard. The August date for school opening comes and goes without a child appearing. All of September comes and goes without a child. They are confined to their homes by law, quarantined because of the polio epidemic sweeping across the nation. The disease creeps through community after community, reaching into homes and indiscriminately selecting one or two children to infect, to paralyze, or to kill. Even mountain isolation cannot protect their children. Madison County Health Department officials declared a state of emergency. Those under the age of sixteen must remain at home until further notice. No school. No visiting friends. No Sunday School or worship services. Stay home and pray.

My family takes precautions beyond prayer. For example when my uncle, Roscoe Hicks, comes from Newport News with mother's sister and his son to buy a car here, I ride home with them. My Aunt Dory makes her husband Uncle Roscoe roll the windows up because of polio.

On October fourth, school opens when no new cases have been reported in the county. Roaring Fork Elementary School teacher Minnie Ebbs waits by the door for her students on this unusual first day of school. As in the other outlying schools, there remains no electricity, no lunchroom, no library, nor are their indoor bathroom facilities at Roaring Fork School. The only teacher in the two room, three grade school, Mrs. Ebbs also serves as principal and custodian. With eight pupils enrolled in first grade, eleven in second and six in third, she faces the year with twenty-one years of experience. Each year she successfully sends students beginning with the fourth graders to Spring Creek School to continue their education with her instructions as a foundation. Only the very youngest remain here with her in the community.

1949 — Electricity at Spring Creek School broadens the opportunities available to students, although daily lighting still depends on sunlight filtering through several full length windows in each classroom. The single bulb hanging in the center of the room offers little supplemental light and is used mostly on cloudy days. The school adds shades to the auditorium so films can be shown on the newly installed screen. Teachers attend training sessions about how to use the new technology. The lunchroom installs a Frigidaire cooler. However, meals continue to be prepared on a wood cookstove.

Even before the addition of electricity, the high school had been the center of recreation and entertainment for sporting events in the area. Other than baseball, these were night time activities so outsiders could attend. Electricity now makes lighting available for high school basketball games or for cake walk socials or for the many country and blue grass music bands that are so abundant. Renowned speakers are invited, and speaking contest between students are held occasionally. A sixteen mm movie is often shown for entertainment and to raise money for the school. Most of these activities are fundraising events, and ten cents is the usual charge for students.

The high school introduces a new drivers' education program with a training car. Bernard Brigman reduces his class load to four hours per day to devote more time to his duties as principal.

The school population increases at Meadow Fork School to over a hundred twenty students and a fourth teacher is added, Nina Balding, a first year teacher with a "C" level wartime certification. The continual lack of instructional equipment contributes to the unaccredited classification of the school.

Meadow Fork School and Church photo courtesy of Spring Creek Community Center

1950 — Home Economics and Typing are added to the curriculum as well as Vocational Agriculture and "Shop" with an emphasis on woodworking and furniture. Earlier precautions to prevent flooding in the basement of the school prove futile and a new ditch is cut behind the school. The swamp is again drained and a fence is built around the school.

1951 — Up to this date the cafeteria has been a part of the actual school building. This year a separate facility to house a cafeteria is built in the previous location of the janitor's house behind the school.

1954 — Children in the Spring Creek community are standing in line in the gymnasium of the school. Ahead of them is a nurse overseeing the local battle against polio. She makes sure each and every child receives a shot, dose number one of the Salk vaccine, the first step to eradicate polio in the valley. Other doses will follow. Polio is conquered.

The early fifties — Small schools in the community are consolidated into Spring Creek, first by closing Meadow Fork and Keenerville, and then later, Roaring Fork.

Somewhere in the fifties — Life at Spring Creek School continues not as affected by the outside world, but more influenced by daily events. With no telephone available to notify a parent when a child gets sick at school, the principal (who is also a part time teacher) gives his class an assignment, leaves the grounds, and takes the sick child home. He appoints a student to "take names," but usually that person will not tell on the others no matter what happens.

On one such day, reports a class member, as soon as he leaves to perform this duty, the students in his class all put a wad of chewing tobacco in their mouths, courtesy of one of the girls in class who chews. They miss timing his return, and he walks into the classroom before the students have a chance to spit their wads out. They get sick and by the time recess comes, they are rolling on the grass.

A hickory tree in the side yard of school becomes a gathering spot for smokers of all ages where many younger children begin their smoking habits from watching older students. This is a tobacco growing community. There are no school rules about smoking.

The hickory tree becomes a favorite spot for others as well. With no money to purchase a baseball, the younger boys devise their own. They crack the hickory nut shells open with two rocks and with their knives they gouge out the round nut inside. They wrap thread around the hickory nut until it becomes the size of a baseball. Then they use glue or tape to hold it together and form a ball to play baseball.

On October 15 of each year the school closes for the first day of squirrel season, as "Everyone would have laid out anyway." On other days during the season, bus drivers pick up the squirrel hunters carrying their guns.

One teacher who uses a crutch because he has only one leg still manages to drive one of the school buses. In fact, he can do more with a crutch than anyone can imagine, fishing, climbing over rocks. He often picks up my father in his A-model Ford and takes him on house calls. He delights the students by assigning each one a rhythmic nickname and most of them wonder if he even knows their real, given names. Sadly he mentions one day that he is not feeling well and he rests on the bench outside the principal's office. He has a massive heart attack and dies there at the school.

The sixties — After the bus pulls into the school, the children remain in their separate classrooms rather than going to an assembly as in earlier years. In June of 1963 the United States Supreme Court ruled in favor of Madalyn Murry O'Hair's lawsuit stating the Baltimore City Public School System requiring her child to read the Bible at school is unconstitutional, essentially eliminating prayer or devotions at public schools.

Other daily activities continue unchanged. As in the tradition of the years before them, the seventh graders perform a May pole dance on the front lawn decorating with crepe paper. The girls wear white blouses and pastel colored skirts. Their teacher, Mrs. Price, discovers an old long playing record of a French minuet with an instruction sheet for the classes to attempt to learn and perform in front of the school and parents.

During recess the children play unorganized activities, grammar grades going outside first. The teachers sit on the sidelines and watch without interfering. The children know each other across the grade levels and get along like a family. This is home schooling in the school.

Because there is no telephone in the school, innovative ways of communication with the outside world become necessary. One particular teacher's children are infants and often need help only their mother can give. Since her classroom windows face her home across the flats, the sitter hangs a diaper on the front porch as a signal for her to come home immediately.

Jokesters abound at the school carrying on the tradition of the mountain people. A biology teacher and a student one day make a scheme discussing their plans at lunch break. During class that afternoon the student and teacher begin "arguing." The teacher opens his desk drawer and pulls out a starter pistol. He aims at the student and fires. The student pretends he is hit, dramatically grabs his chest and falls to the floor. Before they can tell the class it is a hoax, the girls flee to the bathroom.

1972 — Yearly class reunions begin, allowing all former students and teachers to reconnect.

1974 — The final Spring Creek High School class celebrates high school graduation. A new consolidated high school will open in the fall and offer Spring Creek students a much expanded curriculum. Students in the newly developed kindergarten through those in the eighth grade are to remain in the community at Spring Creek while high school students will be bused to the new Madison County High School.

1989 — Despite the love of the community for Spring Creek School and numerous pleas to save it, dwindling population and falling enrollment lead to its demise. Much needed repairs and updates to the school building prove too costly and not economically feasible. Madison County officials make the decision to close the school and bus the remaining kindergarten through eighth graders down Highway #209 to Hot Springs Elementary School.

The time is somewhere in the mid-nineties — Local citizens band together to bring the school back to life. The group walks through the school to determine the feasibility of refurbishing the dilapidated school building. The roof has deteriorated and the interior is nearly destroyed as a result, yet they envision a much needed community center or library. Under the leadership of Jack Woody and J. D. Waldroup, the group begins the fund raising process by writing grants. The first order of business is to restore the roof to protect the school itself. After that, renovations can begin. Also in there working to raise money are Layton Davis, Mary Ruth Fowler and Dean Justice.

This group, along with Christine Grasty as treasurer, has constituted the executive committee, and what a great group they are!! They have already learned that government funds are available for refurbishing old schools and historic sites. They have already submitted several applications and have one matching grant approved to total $20,000, dollar for dollar.

Raising money is hard. We look into many possibilities, but we receive little financial help from local people to start with. They are still the same mindset like years before in Madison when money was a scarce item and when they did not need too much money because they were self-sufficient. Back then, neighbors helped neighbors. When they got sick, neighbors came in. But this is different, this is now. We need some money and we find money is hard to get. The community people willingly come to work all day, just like in the old days, as a neighbor, and not charge anything for their services, but when we ask them to borrow a dollar, that is different. We need to get more enthusiasm fired up to complete this matching grant.

Our plan is to first get the community interested in the project and excited to give money. Some who have a little extra money begin to create competition by pledging sizable contributions if and when progression on the grant to a certain point has been reached.

This does the trick! The first grant for ten thousand dollars matches what we raise on our part. When we receive this initial grant money, we install a new roof on the building. Other grant applications begin to be approved and large donations from interested groups, large community yard sales, local musician entertainment, and special meals at the fire department get the entire community involved.

During the interim of annual meetings, Jack Woody has decided to step down as president of the Alumni Association and the executive committee decides that I would be their nominee to succeed Jack. I learn of this "set up" when my wife Helen and I attend the next meeting.

Next we turn our attention to the building. All the floors inside need replaced or refinished, and a campaign set up for donations to replace the gym floor proves to be successful. The doors are replaced by individual purchases that are acknowledged with a plaque. At least half of the windows are broken and those huge, ceiling-tall old windows are expensive to replace. We accomplish that by offering a memorial plaque to place at each window recognizing donations given to honor people. The gym is one of last projects we look to complete.

At first we want to use the agricultural building that was added in the late fifties, but we find it to be beyond repair and we have to tear it down. We add a new heating system so we are able to use the building in winter as well as in summer.

August 9, 1998 — The county signs the school over to the Spring Creek Community Center.

The twenty-first century — The school building is in use, just as we have hoped. Joyce Ledford runs a restaurant there for about five years and, like the fund raising projects inside the school, sells recognition boards enough to build a deck outside the front of the school building. We have several possibilities of businesses to use the facility. Right now women in the community have to drive far for a hairdresser, so we're looking to fill that need. Dave Thomas has a popular restaurant, *Dave's 209*, in the rooms that were once high school classrooms.

Hanging on the walls of the interior hall in the center of the school is a gallery of photographs donated by families and individuals that gives a pictorial chronicle our community.

We are now in the process of obtaining donations or a grant for a heating system for the remaining part of the building. We have a fund set up to accept memorial donations.

The cafeteria building has become a food pantry associated with a Feeding America organization out of Asheville, MANNA Food Bank, an acronym for Mountain Area Nutritional Needs Alliance. Sharing that space is an adult nutritional site that serves meals cooked in Marshall, the county seat, and delivered four times a week.

A reunion of former students and teachers continues to be held in July of each year.

Spring Creek School is abandoned no longer.

A much needed fire department, rescue squad and helicopter pad are built adjacent to the school building...my father would be amazed

The deck in front of the school with umbrella tables

Epilogue

Many great things have happened to me in these eighty plus years. But the greatest was when I met and married HELEN LOUISE WHISNANT on July 10, 1954. She was and is a great wife and more especially, a great mother.

The next four greatest were when each of our four boys were born. I could not have asked for a better assortment! No two are alike except in physical appearance and each is great in his own way! They love their mother and me, and each other!

The next four greatest turned out to be when each of the boys picked a great lady for a wife! They have become the daughters we never had. We love them as if they were our very own!

The next twelve greatest are the Grand and Great-Grand Children! They can't help but become good people! My greatest achievement by far is my family! *The Powers that Be* have smiled on me!

Other than my family, if I have done anything to make things better in this world, it was as an educator. I taught all ages of students to learn everything they possibly could in every field of knowledge and to think independently for themselves, just like the lessons I learned back in the time I grew up in the isolation of these Madison County mountains!

Acknowledgements

Many people helped collect information for this book. Thanks go to members of the Spring Creek Community Center and the Spring Creek Alumni Association for their help. Several of the photographs we included are now found in the main hall of the school. We truly appreciate the center sharing them with us.

Special thanks to Dave Thomas, Christine Grasty, Lottie Mae Gregory, Wilma Reese Wilson, Shirley Clark Ledford, Hazel Thomas, Ruby Price, Ronnie Dale Caldwell, Dean Reeves, Betty Fleming Reeves, Esta Lee King, Lou Askew Reeves, Ethel Meadows Kirkpatrick, Layton Davis, James Ferguson, Mark Ferguson, Tina Bryant, Van Griffith, Major Jean Frese of the Salvation Army, Patrick Cash of the Ramsey Center at Mars Hill University, Diane Richard of Mosaic Research and Project Management, Scenic Byway Coordinator Connie Morgan, and many others who shared with us bits and pieces of their memories.

About the Co-author

Although co-author Gretchen Griffith is not from the Spring Creek Community, her heart has now found a special place to love and appreciate.

Originally from the mountains of western Pennsylvania, she grew up in the North Carolina Piedmont town of Winston-Salem, but found her way back to the mountains as a student at Appalachian State University in Boone, North Carolina. She and her husband, Van, live in the Blue Ridge foothills where she taught fourth graders as they raised a family. She considers herself a "storycatcher" and finds joy in preserving local history. Contact her at www.gretchengriffith.com.

Books

- *Back in the Time: Medicine, Education and Life in the Isolation of Western North Carolina's Spring Creek* with Jasper B. Reese
- *Lessons Learned: The Story of Pilot Mountain School*
- *Called to the Mountains: The Story of Jean L. Freese*
- *When Christmas Feels Like Home*
- *Wheels and Moonshine: The Stories and Adventures of Claude B. Minton* with Johnny Mack Turner
- *Hoop Hike*
- *Fly Fishermen of Caldwell County, North Carolina: Life Stories* with Ron Beane
- *Gracie's Grumpy Grandma*
- *Racing On and Off the Road in Caldwell County and Surrounding Areas* with Johnny Mack Turner

Made in USA - Crawfordsville, IN
14701_9781542858557
10.29.2020 1528